Park

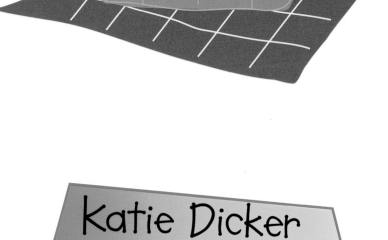

Katie Dicker

Cherrytree Books are distributed in the United States
by Black Rabbit Books, P.O. Box 3263, Mankato, MN 56002

Library of Congress Cataloging-in-Publication Data

Dicker, Katie.
  Park / Katie Dicker.
      p. cm. -- (Sparklers out and about)
  Includes index.
  ISBN 978-1-84234-611-2 (library binding)
  1. Parks--Juvenile literature. I. Title. II. Series.

  SB481.3.D53 2011
  712'.5--dc22

                                    2009044998

First Edition
9 8 7 6 5 4 3 2 1

First published in 2009 by Evans Brothers Ltd.
2A Portman Mansions, Chiltern Street, London W1U 6NR, United Kingdom

Produced for Evans Brothers Limited by
White-Thomson Publishing Ltd

Contents

Park Time

Come and play in the park!

How high can YOU jump?

skip!

5

On the Grass

springy!

The grass is soft to lie on.

I'm a shadow!

What patterns can YOU make on the grass?

Follow the Path

spring blossom

Flat paths are good for biking.

This footpath is covered with fallen leaves.

9

vein →

What's the LARGEST
leaf you can find?

11

By the Pond

How far can YOUR boat sail?

ripple

What do ducks like to eat?

Quack!

13

Walk the Dog

Woof!

Harvey loves to go to the park.

Wait for me!

How fast can YOU run?

Footprints

Can you find the animals' footprints?

What marks do YOU leave behind?

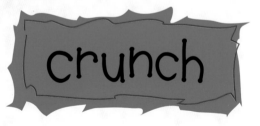

crunch

17

Picnic Time

Yum!

What picnic food do YOU like to eat?

Take an **umbrella** in case it rains!

19

At the Playground

Hi!

The playground is full of new friends to meet.

What's YOUR favorite playground ride?

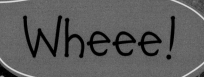

Wheee!

Notes for Adults

Sparklers books are designed to support and extend the learning of young children. The books' high-interest subjects help ease children's transition from home life to the school environment.

Themed titles
Park is one of four **Out and About** titles that encourage children to explore outdoor spaces.
The other titles are:
Garden   **Beach**   **Woods**

Making the most of reading time
When reading with younger children, take time to explore the pictures together. Ask children to find, identify, count, or describe different objects. Point out colors and textures. Allow quiet spaces in your reading so that children can ask questions or repeat your words. Try pausing mid-sentence so that children can predict the next word. This sort of participation develops early reading skills.

Follow the words with your finger as you read. The main text is in Infant Sassoon, a clear, friendly font designed for children learning to read and write. The labels and sound effects add fun and give the opportunity to distinguish between levels of communication. Where appropriate, labels, sound effects, or main text may be presented phonically. Encourage children to imitate the sounds.

As you read the book, you can also take the opportunity to talk about the book itself with appropriate vocabulary such as "page," "cover," "back," "front," "photograph," "label," and "page number."

You can also extend children's learning by using the books as a springboard for discussion and further activities. There are a few suggestions on the facing page.

Pages 4–5: Park Time
Draw a large park scene or cut out a photograph from a magazine. Make a collection of labels with park words and encourage children to help you to stick them to the appropriate parts of the picture — such as grass, path, trees, playground, bench, lake, trash can. Talk to children about the expanse and variety of a park area and the different types of games that can be played there.

Pages 6–7: On the Grass
Children may enjoy sitting or lying on an expanse of dry grass. Encourage them to describe what it feels and smells like. Help a group of children to make patterns of their own on the grass, such as making flower shapes or forming shadows in the sunlight.

Pages 8–9: Follow the Path
Draw a simple maze and encourage children to follow the paths to get to the fountain (or treasure!). Talk to children about good reasons to stick to the paths in a park (to avoid muddy grass and to keep off flowerbeds, for example) and why paths are good for activities on wheels. Encourage children to be aware of the needs of other park users when they explore a park for themselves.

Pages 10–11: Trees and Leaves
Collect a selection of leaves from a local park and encourage children to group them in order of size. Use books or the Internet to help the children identify which trees they are from. Encourage children to compare and contrast the different leaves. What color are they? What do they feel like?

Pages 12–13: By the Pond
Help children to make their own boat or raft made from paper or twigs. Sail the boats on a nearby pond or a large pool of water. Which model boats are the best at sailing and why? How are they affected by the weather conditions? Children may also enjoy trying to stand on one leg like a duck.

Pages 14–15: Walk the Dog
Children may enjoy making their own sausage dog with modeling balloons. See for example, www.ehow.com/video_4411954_tie-balloon-animals.htm for ideas. Encourage children to find pictures of different types of dogs using books, magazines, or the Internet to help them to become more familiar with dogs they may meet in a park.

Pages 16–17: Footprints
Children may enjoy making their own footprints on paper using nontoxic craft paints. Make a collage of the footprints on the wall. Who has the largest footprint? Who has the smallest?

Pages 18–19: Picnic Time
Encourage children to think of a menu for a park picnic. Talk to children about the importance of a balanced diet and what makes good picnic food. Children may enjoy having an indoor mini picnic of their own, sitting on a blanket and sharing pieces of fruit, for example.

Pages 20–21: At the Playground
Draw an outline of a park playground and encourage children to color in the different rides. Which rides are their favorite? Talk to children about using the playground safely and helping to keep it a pleasant place for other children, by throwing away litter, for example. Children may enjoy designing a poster about keeping a park clean and tidy.

Index

Picture acknowledgements:
Alamy: 12 (Glenn Harper), 15 (Andrew Linscott); **Corbis:** cover boy (Moodboard), 4 (Randy Faris), 5 (AKIRA/amanaimages), 6 (Simon Jarratt), 11 (image100), 14 (Ron Chapple), 17 (KAZUO OGAWA/amanaimages); **Getty Images:** 7 (Martin Barraud), 9 (Andrew Olney), 10 (Steven Puetzer); **IStockphoto:** cover grass, cover sky (JLFCapture), 8 (Hans F. Meier), 20 (Thomas Perkins); **Photolibrary:** 19 (Robert Llewellyn); **Shutterstock:** cover swing, cover tree (Jan Martin Will), 2–3 grass (Smit), 13 (Sonya Etchison), 16 duck (Goran Kuzmanovski), 16 dog (Ferenc Szelepcsenyi), 16 squirrel (Eric Isselée), 16 pigeon (innocent), 16 footprints (Bill Heller), 18 (iofoto), 21 (Rossario), 22–23 grass (Smit), 24 grass (Smit).